LEGO NEXO KNIGHTS™

MEET THE KNIGHTS

Written by Julia March

DK

Penguin
Random
House

Editor Pamela Afram
Project Art Editor Jon Hall
Designer Jade Wheaton
Pre-Production Producer Siu Yin Chan
Producer Louise Daly
Managing Editor Paula Regan
Managing Art Editor Guy Harvey
Art Director Lisa Lanzarini
Publisher Julie Ferris
Publishing Director Simon Beecroft

Reading Consultant
Linda B. Gambrell, Ph.D

First American Edition, 2016
Published in the United States by
DK Publishing
345 Hudson Street, New York, New York 10014

Page design copyright © 2016
Dorling Kindersley Limited
DK, a Division of Penguin Random House LLC

16 17 18 19 10 9 8 7 6 5 4 3 2 1
001–288030–March/2016

Copyright © 2016 Dorling Kindersley Limited

LEGO, the LEGO logo, NEXO KNIGHTS,
the Brick and the Knob configuration,
and the Minifigure are trademarks
of the LEGO Group.

© 2016 The LEGO Group.
Produced by Dorling Kindersley under
license from the LEGO Group.

All rights reserved. Without limiting the rights
under the copyright reserved above, no part of this
publication may be reproduced, stored in
or introduced into a retrieval system,
or transmitted, in any form, or by any means
(electronic, mechanical, photocopying, recording,
or otherwise), without the prior written
permission of the copyright owner.
Published in Great Britain
by Dorling Kindersley Limited.

A catalog record for this book is available from
the Library of Congress.

DK books are available at special discounts
when purchased in bulk for sales promotions,
premiums, fund-raising, or educational use.
For details, contact: DK Publishing Special
Markets, 345 Hudson Street, New York, New
York 10014 SpecialSales@dk.com

ISBN: 978-1-4654-4473-8 (Hardback)
ISBN: 978-1-4654-4474-5 (Paperback)

Printed and bound in China

www.LEGO.com
www.dk.com

A WORLD OF IDEAS:
SEE ALL THERE IS TO KNOW

LEGO® NEXO KNIGHTS™: MERLOK 2.0

Free app · Kostenlose App · Appli gratuite
App gratis · App Grátis · Ingyenes alkalmazás

Device check: Gerät prüfen: Vérification du dispositif:
Comprueba tu dispositivo: Verificação do dispositivo:
Eszközellenőrzés: **LEGO.COM/devicecheck**

Each of the knights has a Shield Power
you can scan. Here is Axl's:

There are four other scannable shields within
the pages of this book—can you find them?

Contents

Welcome to Knighton

The land of Knighton is a mix of old and new. Knights wear high-tech armor and play computer games. Castles stand side by side with movie theaters and shopping malls. The kingdom is ruled by King and Queen Halbert.

GRADUATION DAY

Five young pages have graduated from The Knights' Academy. All of the knights are very different. Each one has promised to protect Knighton from danger.

Clay

Clay wants to be the best knight ever. He trains for hours and hours every day. He has learned the Knights' Code by heart, too. No wonder Clay was top of the class at The Knights' Academy.

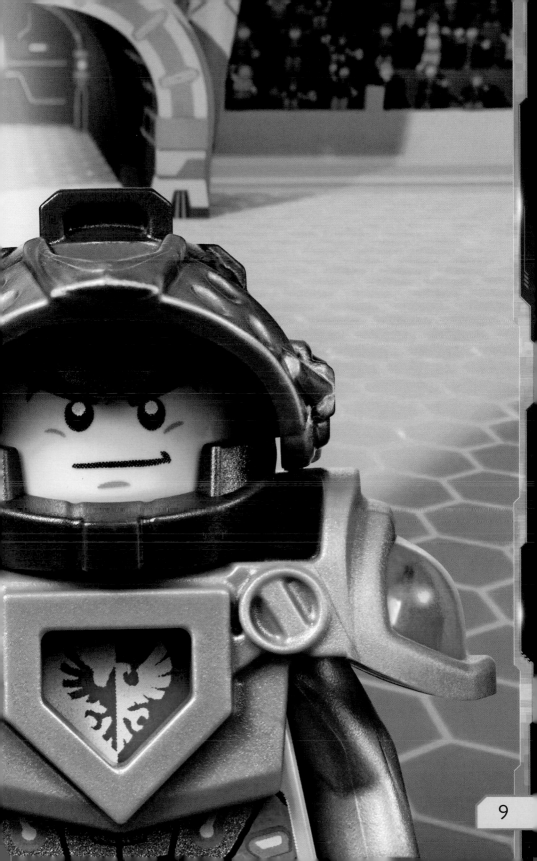

Lance

Lance is a bit of a show-off. He loves to look good. Lance makes sure his armor is extra shiny. He spends lots of money on armor polish. Good thing he is super rich!

Macy

Macy is a princess. She does not like it! Life in the castle is so boring. It is all sparkly dresses and silly dances. Macy cannot wait to be a knight and have adventures.

From: Macy Halbert

Dear Mom,

I just wanted you to know that I am doing great! Now that I am a real knight, I am helping to protect Knighton. I hope Dad will see how good I am at being a knight, too.

We are looking forward to coming to the castle for a big feast. Especially Axl!

Lots of love,

Princess Macy

1 Attachment 📎

Inbox   5 Unread Messages

Sent items

Trash

Contacts

Folders

This is me fighting the Beast Master!

Aaron

Aaron is a thrill-seeker. He loves crazy games and sports. So what if there is a chance things could go wrong? That makes it all the more fun!

Axl

Axl loves to eat. He also loves playing with his band, the Boogie Knights. Axl's favorite song goes like this:

"Oh I am a knight
Who likes a bite
So give me steak,
And beans, and cake!"

Jestro

Jestro is King Halbert's jester.
He does not like being
a jester because people say
he is not very good at it.

Jestro finds some books of dark magic. The king's wizard casts a spell to stop him from using them. KA-BOOM! Jestro and the books are thrown across Knighton.

KNIGHTON

A BLOW FOR JESTRO

The joke really was on Jestro.

NEWS

Hundreds of people came to watch King Halbert's jester, Jestro, perform last night. Jestro's act got plenty of laughs—but only because it all went terribly wrong.

Jestro forgot his jokes. He tripped over his feet. He tried to juggle, but he dropped the balls. The jester even caused a power outage in Knighton. Poor Jestro. What a failure!

The Book of Monsters

Jestro finds the Book of
Monsters. The book wants
to scare people. But first, it needs
help to free the monsters
trapped inside it.

Jestro is mad at everyone who laughed at him. He will help the Book of Monsters scare people!

WARNING!

MAGMA MONSTERS

Monsters have been spotted in the kingdom. Watch out for their fiery weapons and blazing tempers. Citizens of Knighton beware! If you see a Magma Monster... RUN!

HOTHEADED
SPARKKS

THE FEARSOME
FLAME THROWER

SCURRIERS AND GLOBLINS!

MENACING
MOLTOR

THE TERRIBLE
CRUST SMASHER!

Ava and Merlok 2.0

Ava Prentiss is a very smart student at the Knights' Academy. She finds out that the king's wizard, Merlok, has been sucked into the castle's computer system. Now he is Merlok 2.0.
Merlok 2.0 will be able to help the knights protect Knighton!

The Fortrex

Jestro and his monsters
are causing havoc all over
Knighton. The knights must
stop them. They pile their
gear into a rolling castle
called The Fortrex. Merlok
2.0 can come as well.
Hurry up, knights!

INSIDE
THE FORTREX

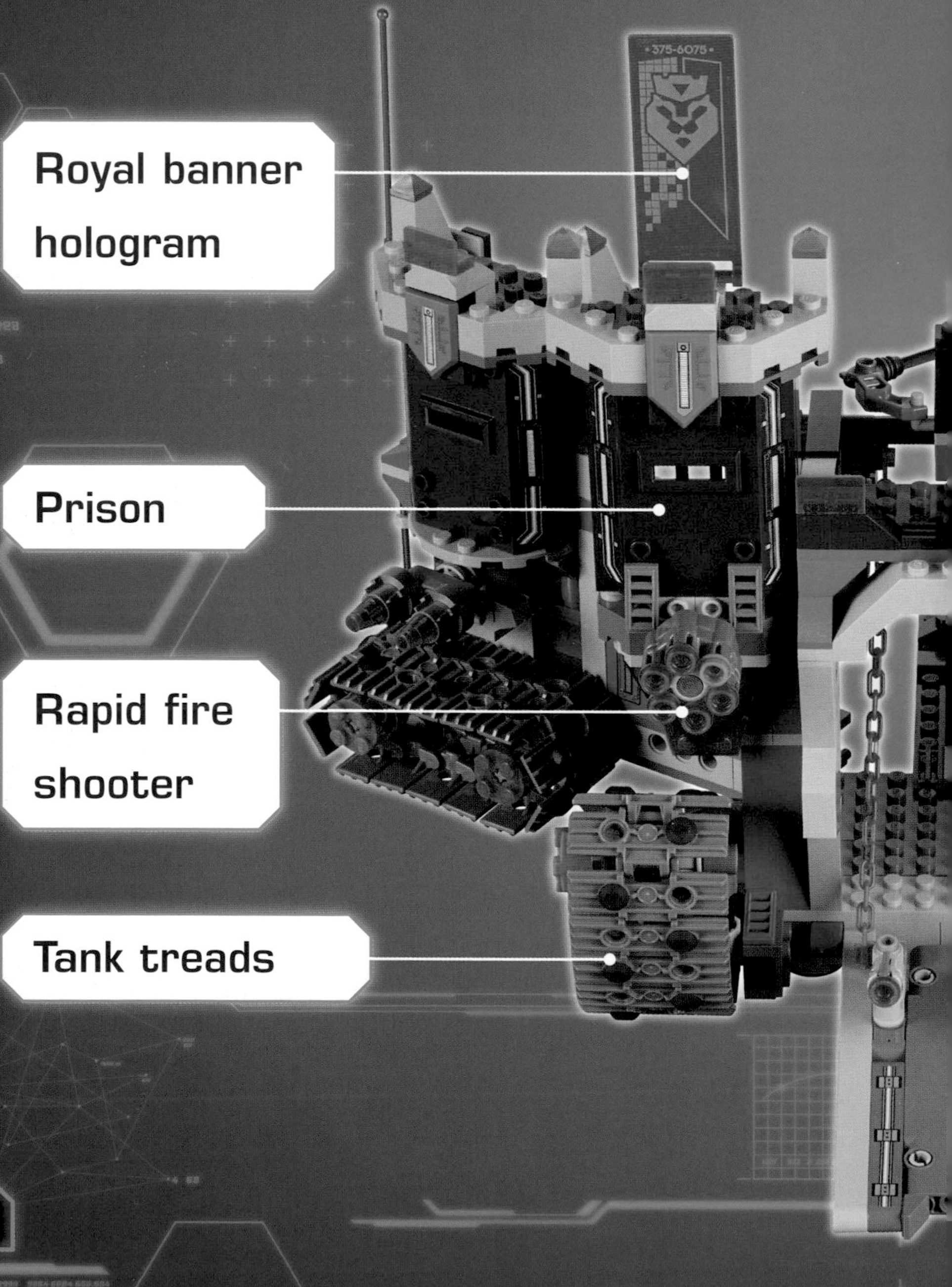

Royal banner hologram

Prison

Rapid fire shooter

Tank treads

375-6075

The Fortrex is like a castle on tank treads. It has a training area for the knights to practice their skills. Merlok 2.0 is part of The Fortrex computer system. He can send powers to the knights' special shields.

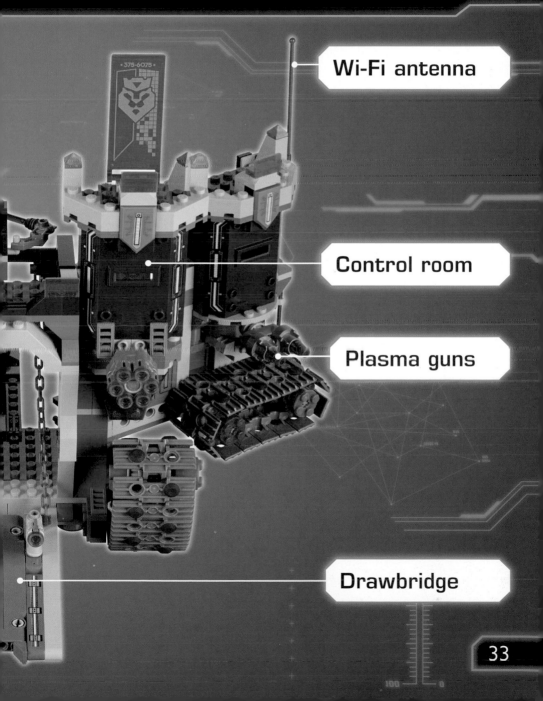

Wi-Fi antenna

Control room

Plasma guns

Drawbridge

NEXO Powers

Merlok 2.0 uploads digital powers to the knights. They are called NEXO Powers. NEXO Powers give the knights special monster-fighting abilities. Their weapons glow bright orange, too. Now they are ready for battle!

"NEXO Powers are great! Clapper Claw allows me to swing my mace with dragon strength!"

POWERS DO?

"Merlok 2.0 sent
Toxic Sting power to my
NEXO Shield. It creates
a cloud of deadly gas.
Watch out, monsters!"

Knights vs. Monsters

The monsters fire their Chaos Catapult at the NEXO KNIGHTS™ heroes. Ouch! But the knights have their own vehicles.

Here comes Clay, driving his Rumble Blade. The monsters do not like the look of that big sword at the front!

Jestro Defeated

The monsters keep attacking Knighton. You can beat them, brave knights!

The knights finally chase off Jestro and his monsters. The King and Queen are so happy. The knights have saved the kingdom.

Quiz

1. Who rules Knighton?

2. Which knight loves crazy games and sports?

3. Why does Macy not like life in the castle?

4. What is the name of King Halbert's jester?

5. What color do NEXO weapons glow?

6. What is the name of the knights' rolling castle?

7. Which knight loves to eat?

8. Who uploads NEXO Powers to the knights?

9. Who drives the Rumble Blade?

10. Which knight keeps his armor extra shiny?

Answers on page 45

Glossary

Academy
A school where people can learn special skills.

Graduate
To successfully complete a course of study.

Havoc
Damage and confusion.

Jester
A servant of a king or queen whose job is to make people laugh.

Mace
A heavy club used as a weapon.

Magma
Melted rock from under the Earth's surface.

Page
Someone who is training to be a knight.

Index

Answers to the quiz on pages 42 and 43:
1. King and Queen Halbert 2. Aaron 3. It is so boring!
4. Jestro 5. Orange 6. The Fortrex 7. Axl 8. Merlok 2.0
9. Clay 10. Lance
Scannable shields can be found on pages 2, 4, 14, 36, and 44.

Guide for Parents

DK Readers is a four-level interactive reading adventure series for children, developing the habit of reading widely for both pleasure and information. These books have an exciting main narrative interspersed with a range of reading genres to suit your child's reading ability, as required by the Common Core State Standards. Each book is designed to develop your child's reading skills, fluency, grammar awareness, and comprehension in order to build confidence and engagement when reading.

Ready for a *Beginning to Read Alone* book
YOUR CHILD SHOULD

- be able to read many words without needing to stop and break them down into sound parts.
- read smoothly, in phrases and with expression. By this level, your child will be beginning to read silently.
- self-correct when a word or sentence doesn't sound right.

A Valuable and Shared Reading Experience

For some children, text reading, particularly non-fiction, requires much effort, but adult participation can make this both fun and easier. So here are a few tips on how to use this book with your child.

TIP 1 Check out the contents together before your child begins:
- Invite your child to check the blurb, contents page, and layout of the book and comment on it.
- Ask your child to make predictions about the story.
- Talk about the information your child might want to find out.

TIP 2 Encourage fluent and flexible reading:
- Support your child to read in fluent, expressive phrases, making full use of punctuation and thinking about the meaning.

- Help your child learn to read with expression by choosing a sentence to read aloud and demonstrating how to do this.

TIP 3 Indicators that your child is reading for meaning:

- Your child will be responding to the text if he/she is self-correcting and varying his/her voice.
- Your child will want to talk about what he/she is reading or is eager to turn the page to find out what will happen next.

TIP 4 Chat at the end of each chapter:

- Encourage your child to recall specific details after each chapter.
- Let your child pick out interesting words and discuss what they mean.
- Talk about what each of you found most interesting or most important.
- Ask questions about the text. These help to develop comprehension skills and awareness of the language used.

A FEW ADDITIONAL TIPS

- Read to your child regularly to demonstrate fluency, phrasing, and expression; to find out or check information; and for sharing enjoyment.
- Encourage your child to reread favorite texts to increase reading confidence and fluency.
- Check that your child is reading a range of different types of material, such as poems, jokes, and following instructions.

- Series consultant, **Dr. Linda Gambrell**, Distinguished Professor of Education at Clemson University, has served as President of the National Reading Conference, the College Reading Association, and the International Reading Association. She is also reading consultant for the **DK Adventures.**

Have you read these other great books from DK?

BEGINNING TO READ ALONE ②

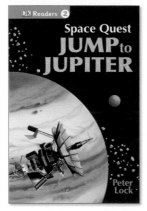

Travel through the asteroid belt to the king of the planets—Jupiter.

Discover how the bravest Ninja in the land save Ninjago.

Meet a host of rebels as they fight for freedom from the Empire.

READING ALONE ③

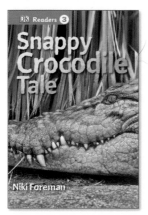

Follow Chris Croc's adventures from a baby to a mighty king of the river.

Follow Batman as he fights to protect Gotham City from crime.

Buckle up and get ready for an action-packed ride!